This book belongs to:

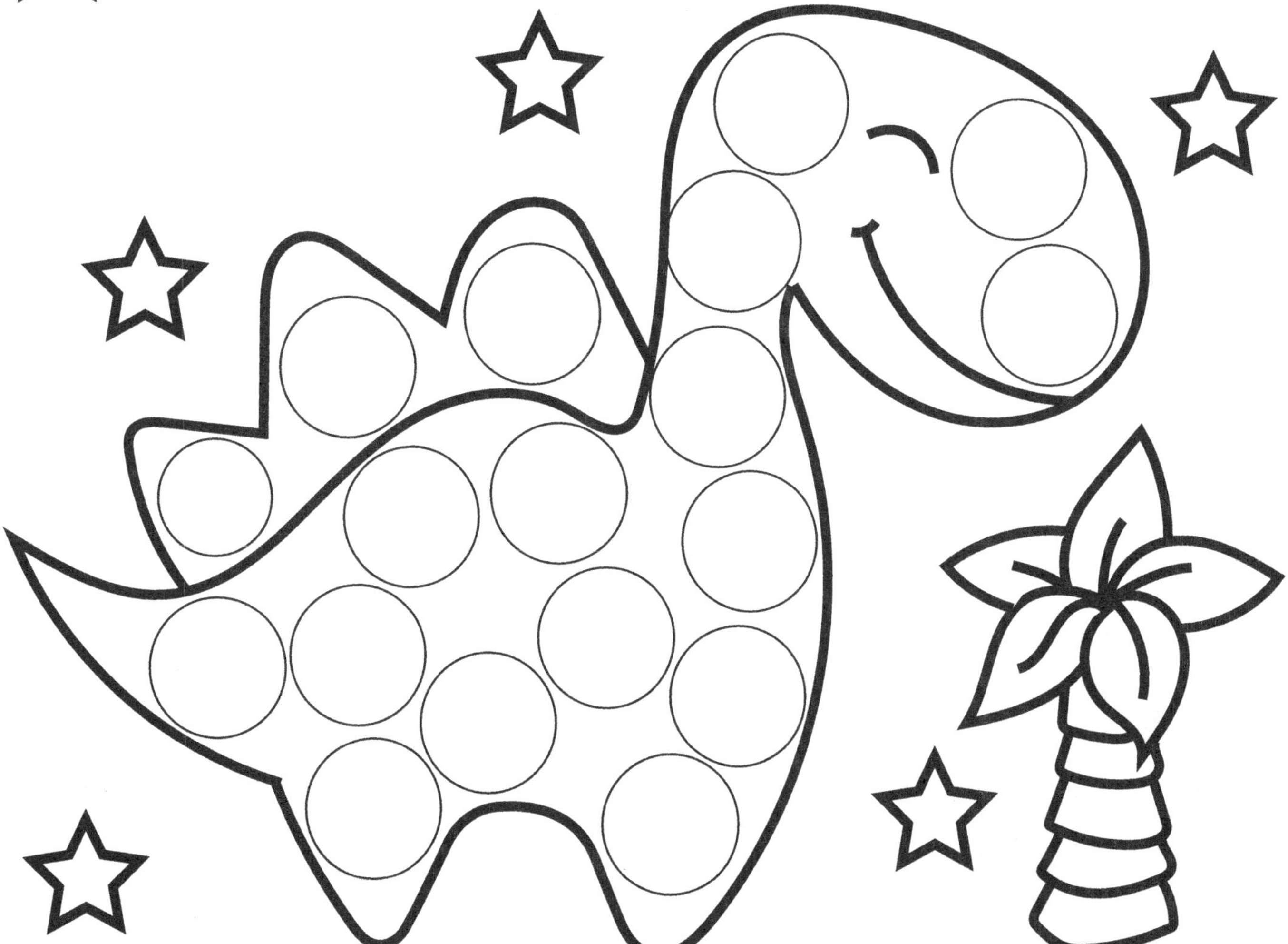

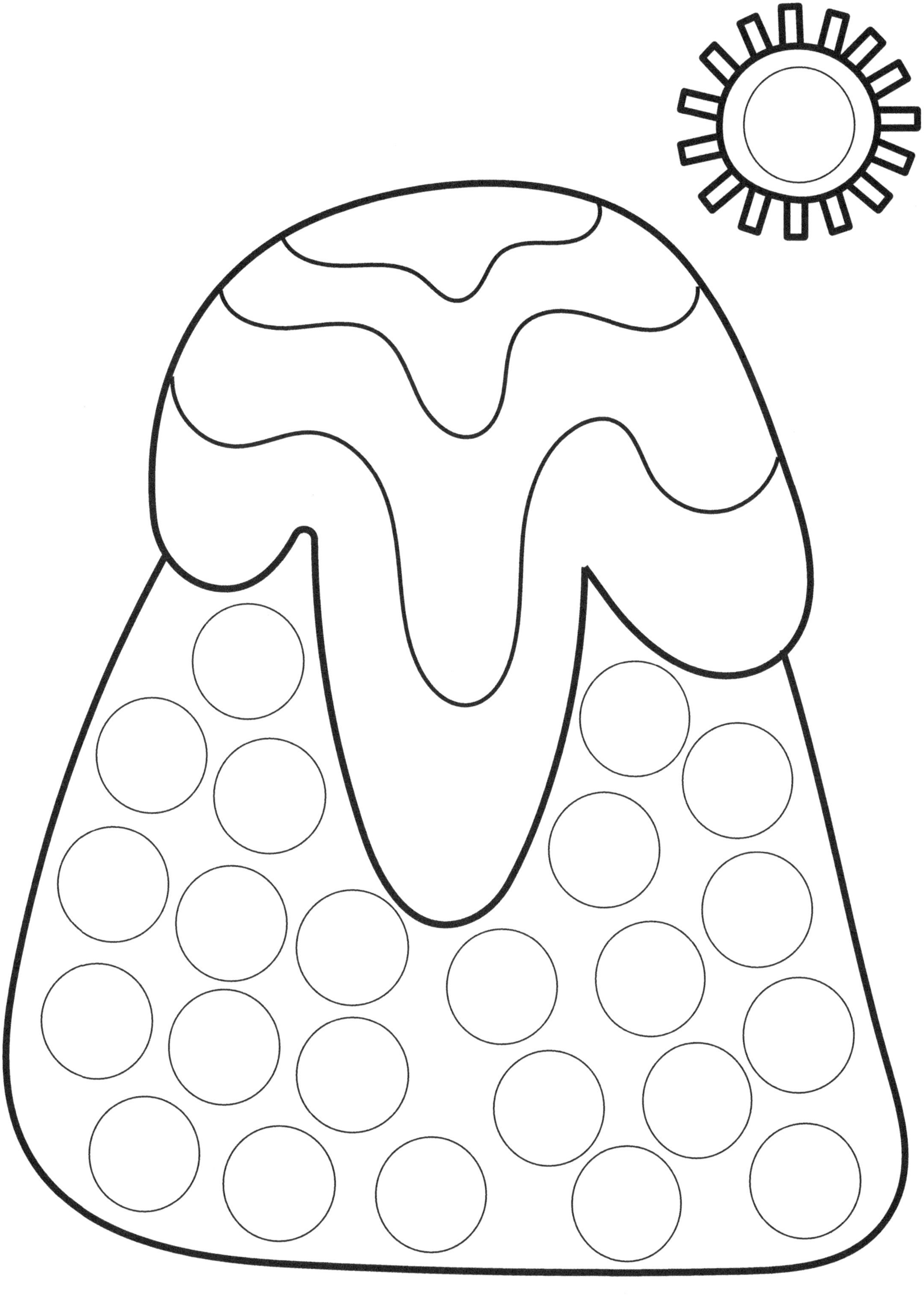

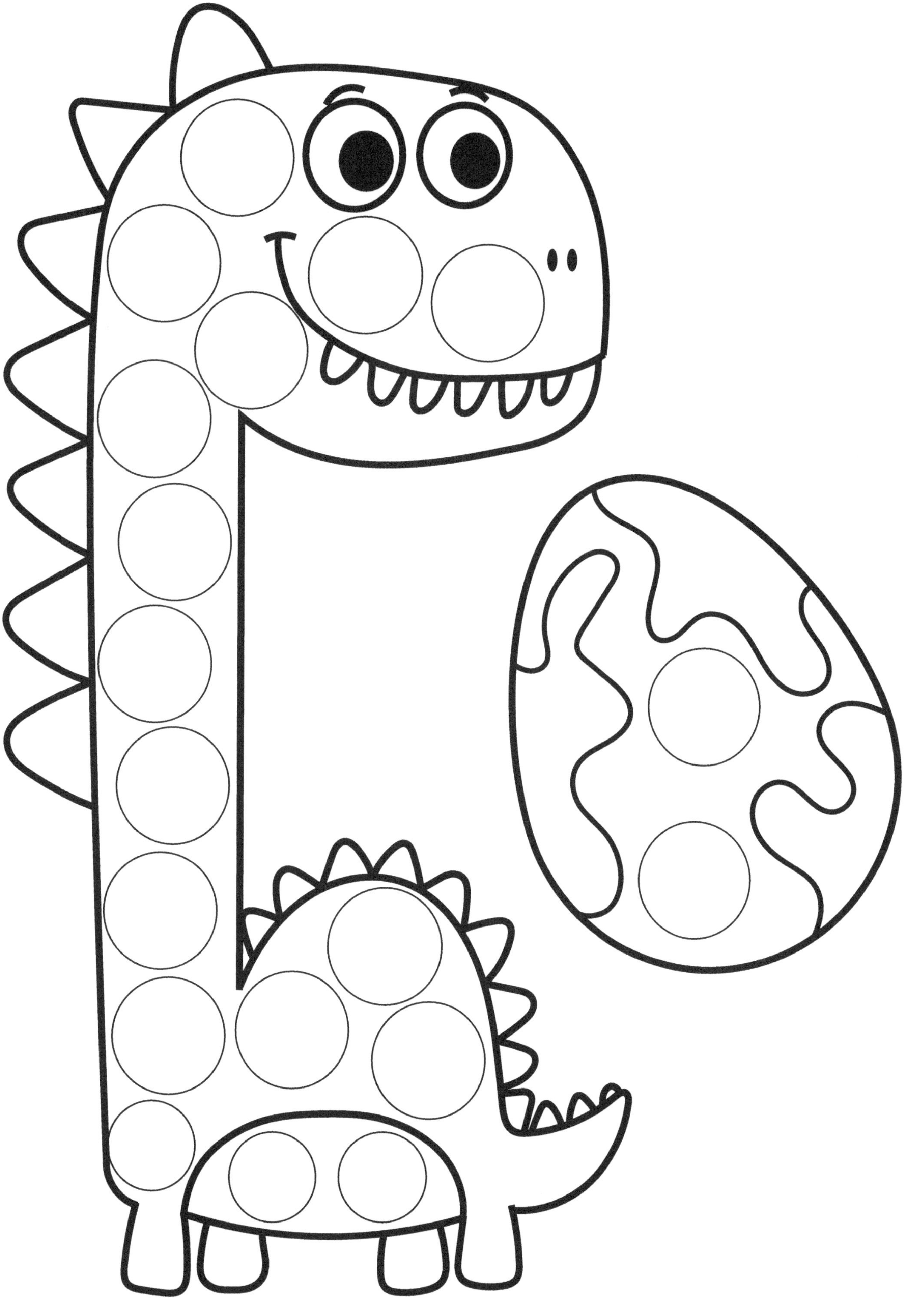

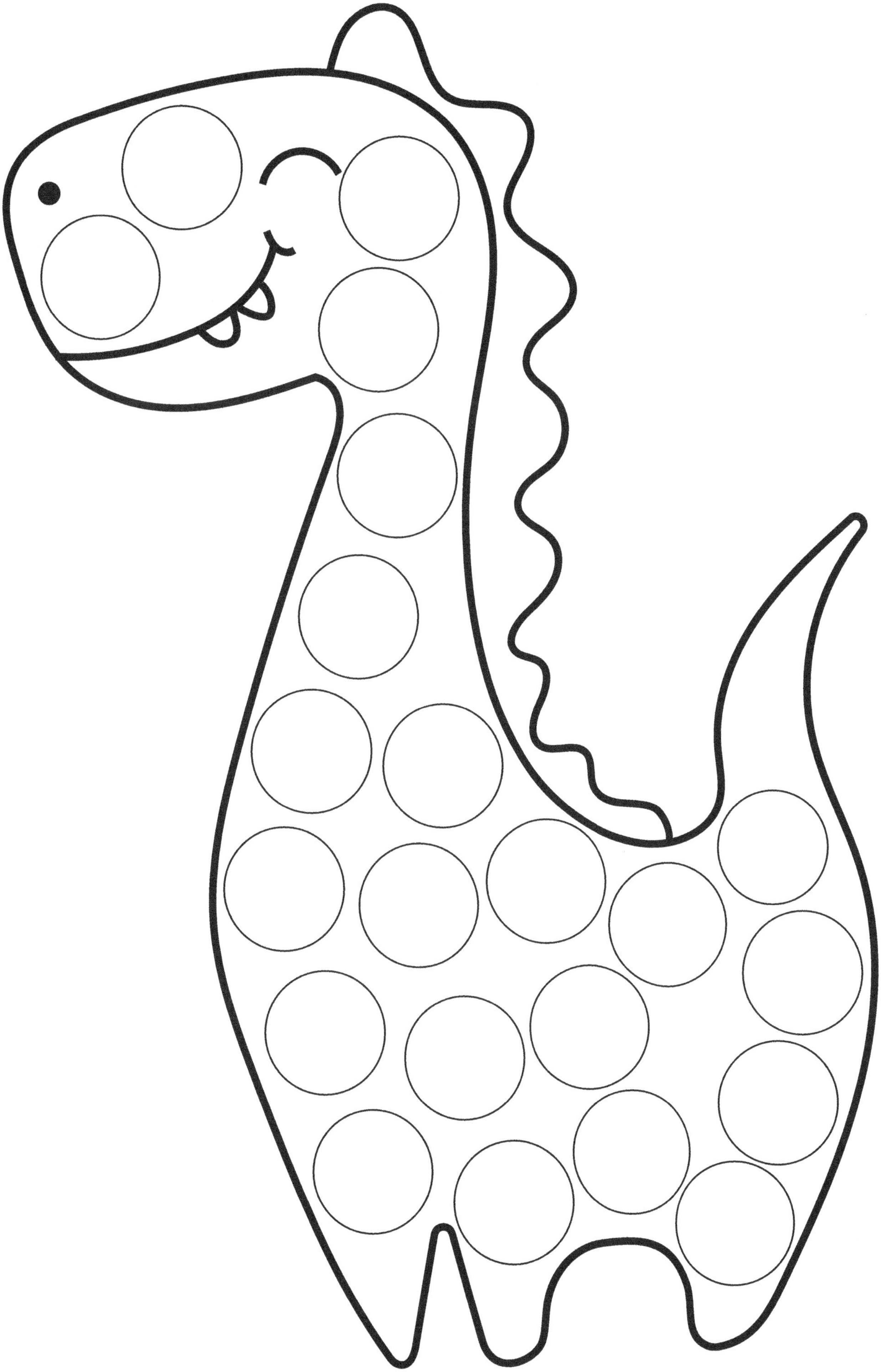

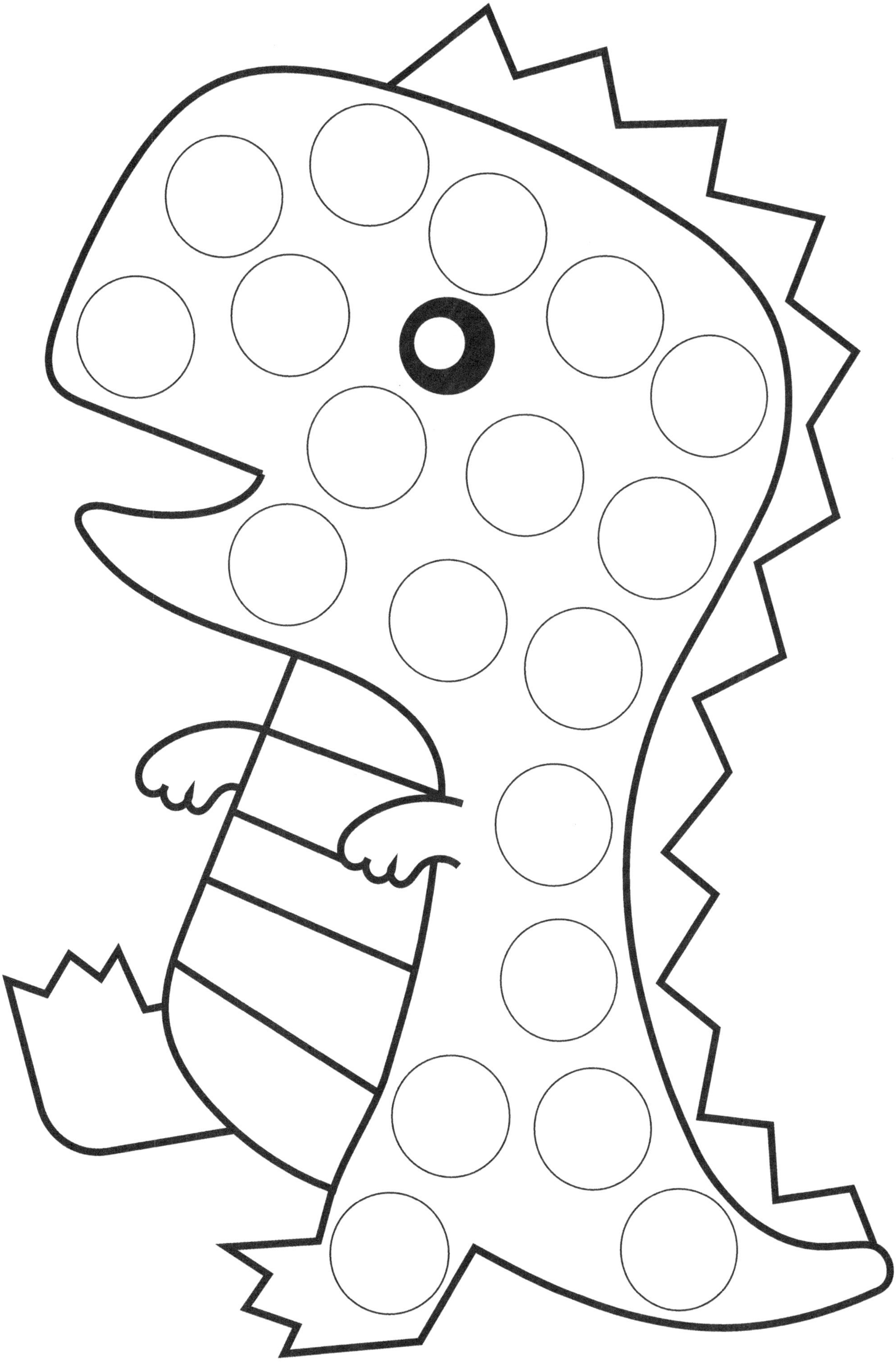

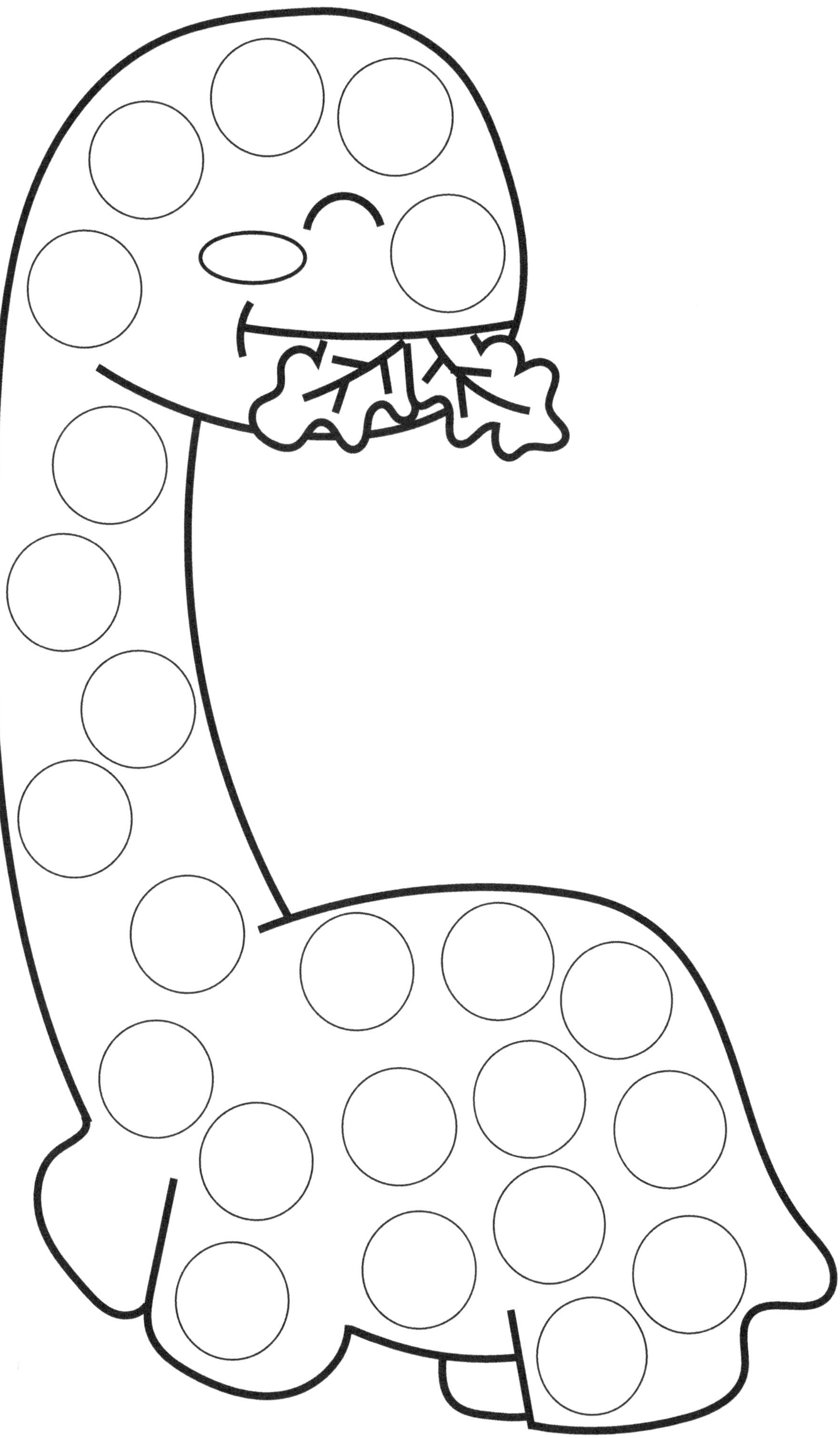

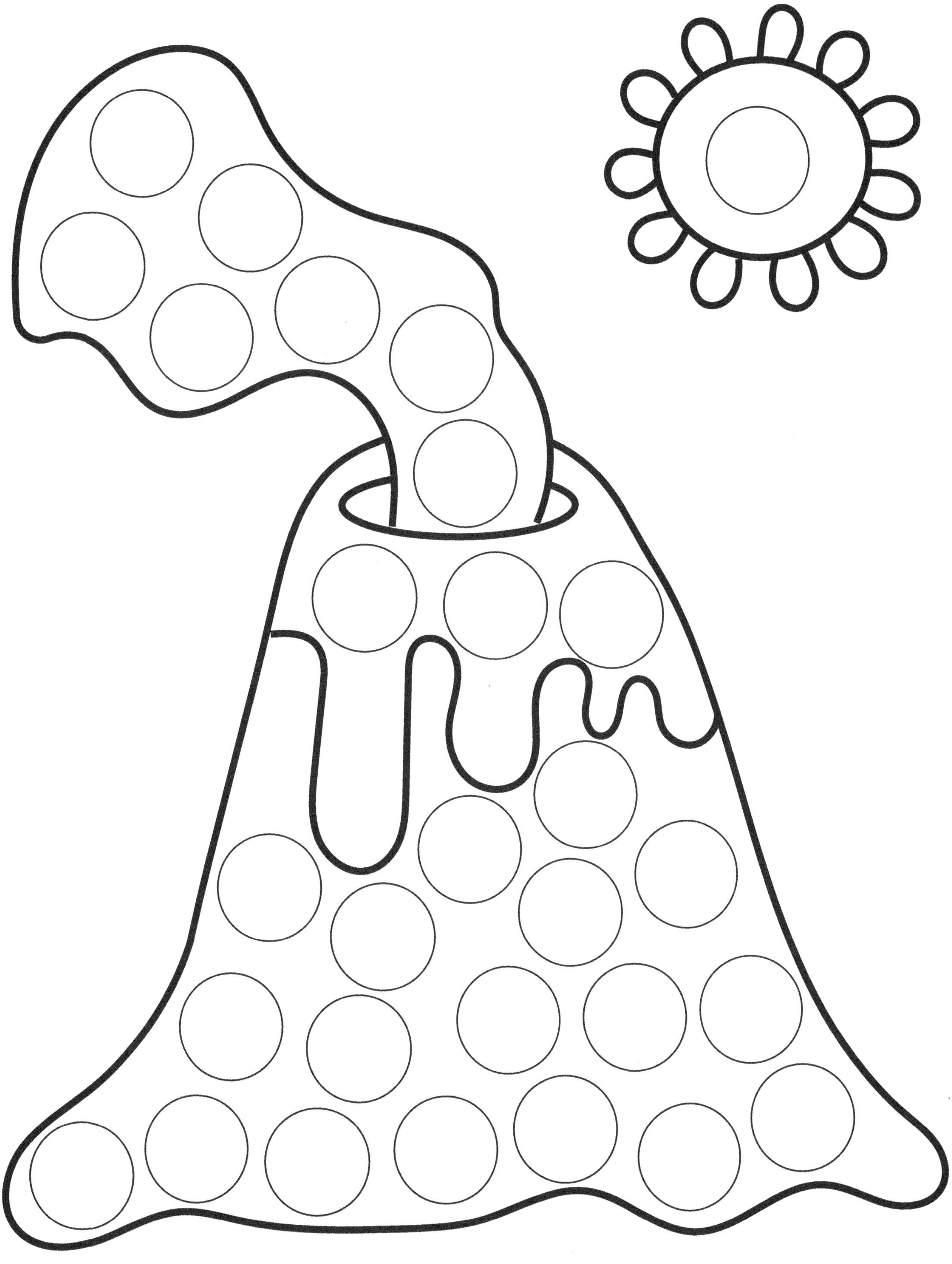

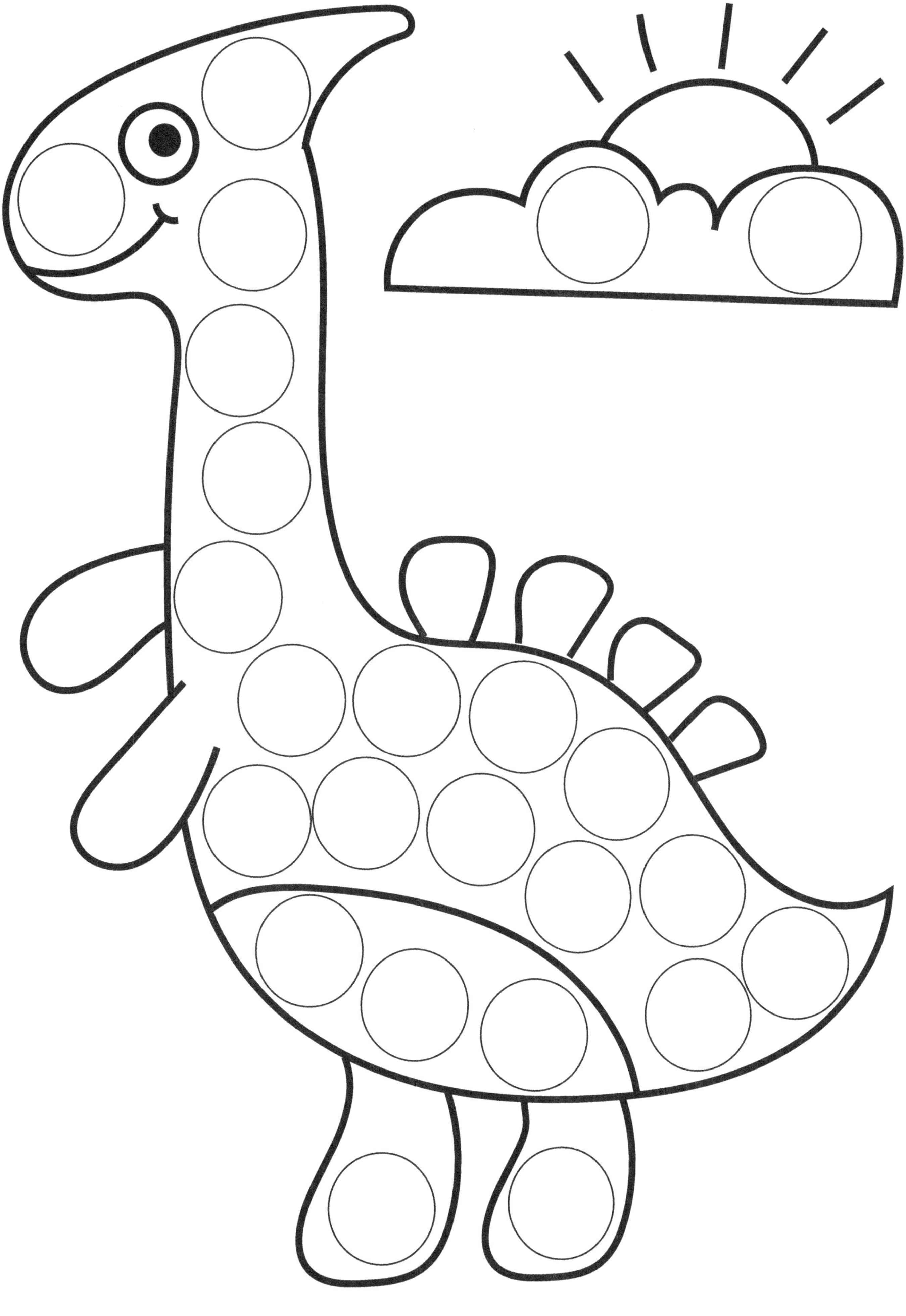

Made in the USA
Las Vegas, NV
19 May 2025

22375307R00059